SUITE FOR THE LIVING

POEMS

MARK NEPO

Grateful acknowledgement is made to following journals and anthologies for first publishing poems from this book:

Apple Farm Poetry Reader (Three Rivers, MI): Practicing, Utterance-That-Rises-Briefly-From-the-Source

Essential Sufism (HarperSanFrancisco): Freefall, God's Wounds, Practicing

Greenfield Review Press, from *Acre of Light*: Endgame, For That, Letter Home, Setting Fires in the Rain, Surviving Has Made Me Crazy, Tu Fu's Reappearance

New Hampshire College Journal: On the Way to Coney Island

Prayers for Healing (Conari Press): Freefall, God's Wounds

Students of the Mystery (Fetzer Institute): Practicing, Utterance-That-Rises-Briefly-From-the-Source, Walking North

Sufi, A Journal of Sufism (London): Before the Twice-Locked Gates, Fighting the Instrument, Freefall, God's Wounds, Walking North

The Patient's Voice: Experiences of Illness (F.A. Davis Co.): The Music Beneath the Music

The Texas Observer: One Step Closer

Published by Bread for the Journey International
Mill Valley, California
415-383-4600
www.breadforthejourney.org

ISBN #: 0-9760575-1-4
Photo: Brandy Sacks

for Susan and Robert,
whose spirits
let me see
my hands
in the dark.

SUITE FOR THE LIVING

PREFACE

The more we live, the less surety we are granted.

Day by day, we stand before what we may never fully comprehend. Life and death, love and loss, wisdom and hope swirl about us as we deftly speed through the obstacles of a life lived in the modern world.

If we are awake, we inevitably find ourselves in the company of things that defy our nimble categories. Persistent mysteries that saturate the world can frighten, confound and confuse our predictable strategies.

But in the company of a poet with clear eyes, we can pierce this mystery and be comforted by the guiding spirit, the hidden wholeness that lives within all things, something glimpsed even before it can be fully known.

Mark Nepo is a generous pilgrim in the landscape of mystery. He lends us his knowing eyes, turning shapes in his capable hands, revealing things we barely know, things that live beneath language. Mark allows them to break surface and here, they breathe.

He reminds us that we know more than we can say and, in times when we need comfort as we need oxygen, we are invited to breathe deeply in love and grace, until we have had our fill.

Mark (and his poetry, for they are as one) has been a loving friend, guide, muse and teacher for countless grateful audiences around the world. Wherever I speak, if I read one of Mark's poems I know to bring many copies, for I will inevitably be asked by hungry listeners for something to take home.

Here, finally, is a glorious collection of some of Mark's poetry, some familiar and beloved, some new and refreshing. They are a string of pearls, a daisy chain of gifts, blessings and treats for the heart.

May you find some comfort here.

— Wayne Muller, California, July, 2004

BREAKING SURFACE

*You didn't come into this house so I might tear off
a piece of your life. Perhaps when you leave
you'll take something of mine: chestnuts,
roses or a surety of roots.*

——*Pablo Neruda*

WHERE NO ONE STAYS A STATUE

It was a sunny day
and I went to the park
and sat on a bench. I was
one of many coming out
from under our rocks
to warm and lengthen.

He was two benches down,
a gentle older man
staring off into the place
between things, beyond
any simple past, staring
into the beginning or the end,
it was hard to say.

When he came up
our eyes met
and he knew I'd seen him
journey there and back.

There was no point in looking away.
And so, he shuffled over
and sat beside me. The sun
moved behind the one cloud
and he finally said
in half a quiver, "How
can we go there together?"

I searched my small mind
for an answer. At this,
he looked away and the sun came out
and I realized this is what the lonely
sages of China were talking about,
what the moon has whispered
before turning full for centuries,
what dancers leap for, what violinists
dream after fevering their last note.

But I was awkward and unsure.
He stared, as if to search my will,
and after several minutes,
he just patted my hand
and left.

I watched him
darken and brighten in the sun
and vowed to look
in the folds of every cry
for a way through
and hoped someday
to meet him there.

THE LESSON

When young, it was the first fall from love.
It broke me open the way lightning splits a tree.
Then, years later, cancer broke me further.
This time, it broke me wider the way a flood
carves the banks of a narrow stream.
Then, having to leave a twenty year marriage.
This broke me the way wind shatters glass.
Then, in Africa, it was the anonymous face
of a schoolboy beginning his life.
This broke me yet again. But this
was like hot water melting soap.

Each time I tried to close
what had been opened.
It was a reflex, natural enough.
But the lesson was, of course, the other way—
in never closing again.

SETTING FIRES IN THE RAIN

You see. It was time. The tube had to come out. It had drained my lung of blood for days, through a slit in my side. The doctor was waiting and I looked to Paul at the foot of my bed. Without a word, he knew. All the talk of love was now in the steps between us. He swept past the curtain. Our arms locked and he crossed over, no longer watching. He was part of the trauma and everything — the bedrail, the tube, my face, his face, the curve of blanket rubbing the tube, the doctor pulling the tube's length as I held onto Paul — everything pulsed. And since, I've learned, if you want to create anything — peace of mind, a child, a painting of running water, a simple tier of lilies — you must crossover and hold. You must sweep past the curtain, no matter how clear. You must drop all reservations like magazines in waiting rooms. You must swallow your heart, leap across and join.

IN MUIR WOODS

Masters of stillness,
masters of light,
who, when cut by something
falling, go nowhere and heal,
teach me this nowhere,

who, when falling themselves,
simply wait to root
in another direction,
teach me this falling.

Four hundred year old trees,
who draw aliveness from the earth
like smoke from the heart of God,
we come, not knowing
you will hush our little want
to be big;

we come, not knowing
that all the work is so much
busyness of mind; all
the worry, so much
busyness of heart.

As the sun warms anything near,
being warms everything still
and the great still things
that outlast us

make us crack
like leaves of laurel
releasing a fragrance
that has always been.

CROSSING SOME OCEAN IN MYSELF

Half a century, and finally,
what I feel is what I say and
what I say is what I mean.

What I mean is that others, so used
to my gargantuan efforts to be good,
don't understand my efforts to be real.
They find me coming up short.

I'm simply burning old masks.
And the next step takes me—
I don't know where—
as it should be—
I don't know—
just that I love who I love.
I listen with my heart.
I struggle with the reflexes of my mind.

I mean, the pains of life are sharper now
but disappear more clearly the way
knives are swallowed by the sea.
And the subtleties of being come on
like waves that cleanse but which,
when dry, cannot be seen.

So much like a gentle animal now,
unsure what I was fighting for,
except to breathe and sing, except
to call out the human names of God
that others have uttered when
thoroughly stripped of their plans.

So much like a love animal now
until the end of any day's work

is the soft moment
when loving and being loved
are the same.

And all year round,
the birds and trees instruct,
make visible the wind
the way reaching without shame
makes visible the love.

FIGHTING THE INSTRUMENT

Often the instruments of change
are not kind or just
and the hardest openness
of all might be
to embrace the change
while not wasting your heart
fighting the instrument.

The storm is not as important
as the path it opens.
The mistreatment in one life
never as crucial as the clearing
it makes in your heart.

This is very difficult to accept.
The hammer or cruel one
is always short-lived
compared to the jewel
in the center of the stone.

BREAKING SURFACE

Let no one keep you from your journey,
no rabbi or priest, no mother
who wants you to dig for treasures
she misplaced, no father
who won't let one life be enough,
no lover who measures their worth
by what you might give up,
no voice that tells you in the night
it can't be done.

Let nothing dissuade you
from seeing what you see
or feeling the winds that make you
want to dance alone
or go where no one
has yet to go.

You are the only explorer.
Your heart, the unreadable compass.
Your soul, the shore of a promise
too great to be ignored.

THE MUSIC BENEATH THE MUSIC

I have tried so hard to please
that I never realized
no one is watching.

I imagined like everyone at school
that our parents were sitting
just out of view like those
quiet doctors behind clean mirrors.

I even felt the future
gather like an audience,
ready to marvel at how much
we had done with so little.

But when I woke bleeding after surgery
with all those mothlike angels
breathing against me, I couldn't
talk and the audience was gone.

I cried way inside and the sobs
were no more than the water
of a deshelled spirit
soaking ground.

Years have passed and I wait
long hours in the sun to see the birch

fall of its own weight into the lake
and it seems to punctuate God's mime.

Nothing sad about it.

And sometimes, at night,
when the dog is asleep
and the owl is beginning to stare
into what no one ever sees,
I stand on the deck and feel
the black spill off the stars,
feel it coat the earth, the trees,
the minds of children half asleep,
feel the stillness evaporate
all notions of fame
into the space
that waits
for light.

Unearthed Again

It starts out simple,
gets complicated and, by
burning what is not real,
gets simple again.

But it's never done.
No matter if we're tired,
spring comes and some undying
impulse needs to break ground.

It's the same with denial,
that winter of the heart. One day,
if blessed, the tulip coated with soil
is again a tulip,
and with an urgency we thought
we left behind, we must wake.

I think we could forget
all the ways to study in school
and just wait for this moment.

Those who wake are the students.
Those who stay awake are the teachers.

It's all as simple, as hard
as staring into ourselves, each other,
this moment
as we would into the sun
until we're blind
until we see.

One Step Closer

I wonder when my father dies
if all the things he couldn't say will fly
out of him, if like a butterfly's wing
in the dark of another continent,
the things he couldn't face
will mount as a wind a
thousand miles away.

I wonder if his gifts
will leave him, too,
if his ability to build
something out of nothing
will spark another's confidence.

I know I was born to say what he couldn't,
to face what he's turned from.
It's the way these things work.
An ecology of spirit.

For instance, a friend has a little girl
just ten months old, and I can tell
by her deep attention that she's
been here before.

I can tell she will say what I cannot
and face what I can't bear.
She stares at me and I stare back,
our eyes sorting what lives, what
breathes, what gives to air.

She still smells the womb-sea and I,
the rocks of this world. She's eager
to be here, though her eyes don't under-
stand the many shades of weight.

But I feel compelled to translate weights
which means I sense the things
that hide in wood and stone,
the things that boil in the pot
of human traffic.

How I make hymns of my father's pain.
How my friend's little girl will make
portraits of how I burn.
This is necessary. It's
how spirit recycles.

We each are born one step closer to God
than those we are born to, for which
we are loved by some and never
forgiven by others.

We each will die with one more thing
to say. We each will wake with
something familiar on our lip
which we must find
and love.

ACCEPTING THIS

Yes, it is true. I confess,
I have thought great thoughts,
and sung great songs—all of it
rehearsal for the majesty
of being held.

The dream is awakened
when thinking I love you
and life begins
when saying I love you
and joy moves like blood
when embracing others with love.

My efforts now turn
from trying to outrun suffering
to accepting love wherever
I can find it.

Stripped of causes and plans
and things to strive for,
I have discovered everything
I could need or ask for
is right here—
in flawed abundance.

We cannot eliminate hunger,
but we can feed each other.
We cannot eliminate loneliness,
but we can hold each other.
We cannot eliminate pain,
but we can live a life
of compassion.

Ultimately,
we are small living things
awakened in the stream,
not gods who carve out rivers.

Like human fish,
we are asked to experience
meaning in the life that moves
through the gill of our heart.

There is nothing to do
and nowhere to go.
Accepting this,
we can do everything
and go anywhere.

LET'S VOICE THE POSSIBILITIES

*I believe what the self-centered
have torn down, the other-centered
will build up.*

—Martin Luther King Jr.

SURVIVING HAS MADE ME CRAZY

I eat flowers now and birds follow me.
I open myself like an inlet
and dolphin energies
swim on through.

Wherever I go, I remain silent
and the silence begins to glow
till one eye in the light
outsees two in the dark.

When asked, I now hesitate
for there are so many ways
to love the earth.

I water things now constantly:
water the hearts of dead friends with light,
the sores of the living with anything warm,
water the skies with a thousand affections
and follow the voices of animals
into grasses that move like ocean.

I eat flowers now and birds come.
I eat care and things to love arrive.
I eat time and as I age
whatever I swallow grows timeless.

I eat and undie
and water my doubts
with silence
and birds come.

WALKING NORTH

No matter how I turn
the magnificent light follows.
Background to my sadness.

No matter how I lift my heart
my shadow creeps in wait behind.
Background to my joy.

No matter how fast I run
a stillness without thought is where I end.

No matter how long I sit
there is a river of motion I must rejoin.

And when I can't hold my head up
it always falls in the lap of one
who has just opened.

When I finally free myself of burden
there is always someone's heavy head
landing in my arms.

The reasons of the heart
are leaves in wind.
Stand up tall and everything
will nest in you.

We all lose and we all gain.
Dark crowds the light.
Light fills the pain.

It is a conversation with no end
a dance with no steps

a song with no words
a reason too big for any mind.

No matter how I turn
the magnificence follows.

THE FIRE THAT TAKES NO WOOD
~ *for Angeles* ~

As a boy I circled a center I couldn't name
and every time I ventured out, I was cut or hit
and thrown back in. As a man, I find life
to be a meeting of centers
and it is the crossing between
that suffers our clumsiness.
It is the crossing
from what I alone experience
to what you alone experience
that set fires in the world,
but once aflame, we are
humbly the same.

No one ever told me
that as snakes shed skin,
as trees snap bark,
the human breast peels,
crying when forced open,
singing when loved open.

And whatever keeps us
from burning truth as food,
whatever tricks the heart into thinking
we can hide in the open, whatever makes us
look everywhere but in the core,

this is the smoke that drives us
from what is living.

And whatever keeps us coming back,
coming up, whatever makes us build a home
out of straw, out of heartache, out of nothing,
whatever ignites us to see again
for the very first time,
this is the bluish flame
that keeps the earth
grinding to the sun.

LOOK AROUND

If you try to comprehend air
before breathing it,
you will die.

If you try to understand love
before being held,
you will never feel compassion.

If you insist on bringing God to others
before opening your very small window of life,
you will never have honest friends.

If you try to teach before you learn
or leave before you stay,
you will lose your ability to try.

No matter what anyone promises—
to never feel compassion,
to never have honest friends,
to lose your ability to try—
these are desperate ways to die.

A dog loves the world through its nose.
A fish through its gills.
A bat through its deep sense of blindness.
An eagle through its glide.

And a human life
through its spirit.

ON THE WAY TO CONEY ISLAND

Eight or nine, rummaging through her basement, through my dead Grandfather's books, when she appeared at the foot of the old see-through stairs, nostalgic and moved that I should be searching through his things. There were no windows and the only light came flooding down the length of stairs over her massive shoulders, giving a sheen to her mat of gray hair. When I turned, she seemed an immigrant deity. I ran to her with this relic, so worn that the cover was indented with a palm print, the edges crumbling like petrified wood. The book seemed very mysterious. The letters were not even in English but in strange and beautiful configurations. She almost cried and sat on the bottom step. I snuggled between her legs, against her apron. She gathered me in as she opened the relic and said, "This was your Grandfather's Talmud. He brought it from Russia." I remember running my little hands all over it the way I do large boulders, trying to feel the years of wind and rain. Her hands were huge and worked, like moveable stones themselves. She turned me by the shoulders, and with the light flooding my face, she whispered, more firmly than I had ever heard anyone whisper, "You are why we came to this country..." She took me by the chin, "You are why I live." She put the relic in my small hands. I was tentative. She gripped me to it firmly and my small palm slid into the well of my grandfather's touch. She stood on the bottom step, blocking the light, "I love you like life itself." She reached down and sandwiched my little fingers, "These are the oldest things you own." As she waddled up the stairs, the light wavered on and off my face. Without turning, she went back to her kitchen. I stood and the light settled in the impression of Nehemiah's grip, a man I never knew, and I didn't want to leave this dungy threshold. I was afraid to climb back into the light. I stood before those stairs, a grimy little innocent, and felt like an orphan who'd been told I was a prince to a kingdom that had perished before I was born. I leafed through the strange letters, watching the light make glitter of the dust. I put the book behind a secret shelf, afraid it would crumble if brought into the world, and walked the lighted stairs, taller than I had descended. I entered her kitchen older yet still a child and climbed her lap like a throne.

THIS IS IT
~ *for Hugh MacLean* ~

He was a Renaissance Scholar,
old school and rigorous,
and of all the night classes
and office summits,
all I can think of
is that day in spring
when he reduced the Trojan War,
the years of death and battle,
to the stealing of a single apple,
a golden apple that couldn't
be eaten anyway.
And before we could bring
into focus what he was suggesting,
he cupped a brass apple
in his wrinkled hand
and said, "This is it."

We all laughed, but
he didn't move or take
his wizened eyes off the brass apple,
and when our minds went silent,
he said with the soft truth of centuries,
"This is it, ladies and gentlemen,
This is it."

I remember the slight dizziness
from just laughing, and how my heart
was pounding, and how I kept flashing —
all our suffering...
from the stealing of an apple
that can't be eaten anyway...
He didn't move, just held
the golden apple before us

with a firm certainty
and no explanation.
It was then that I believed him,
believed him thoroughly…
this was the same apple,
no matter that he brought it
from home, that it weighed him down
all day. I believed him…

That which can't be stolen
but only given,
that which survives
by opening us all,
This is it… here,
underneath every doubt,
in the center of every question,
at the core of all disciplines,
in the silence that outwaits
all smoke and war…
This is it…

And when the barber told me
that my suited Homer had died
before the azaleas saw the sky,
I realized, this is what he taught me…

All study uncovers it.
All love preserves it.
Nothing else matters.
It is the pit inside every moment.

This is it, ladies and gentlemen,
This is it…

THE FEATHER NEVER LANDS

They were the words of a man
who 2600 years ago urged his followers
to rely on their personal experience,
a man whose words have been spun
into 10,000 threads.

I'd waited a long time and searched
for an authentic translation, as if
anything this far down could
resemble his voice, and as I read
in the sun, the soft breeze
unraveled the tensions of my life
and I fell asleep and heard
the lull of an ageless surf,
and he himself came out of the ocean
and we bobbed beyond the breakers,
hardly saying a word, and he merely
ushered me back into my life.

When I woke, I wasn't sure where I was
but the sun through the clouds created
patches of light and dark
that were irresistible
and I began to wonder

why birds sing at the first of light
why crickets cry at the hint of dark
why fish nibble at cracks in the deep.

And so it is ours
to sing and cry and nibble our way free.

Don't ask me why—
Just know that humans
sleep before the truth
and learn it nonetheless.

GOD'S WOUNDS

Through the great pain of stretching
beyond all that pain has taught me,
the soft well at the base
has opened, and life
touching me there
has turned me into a flower
that prays for rain. Now
I understand: to blossom
is to pray, to wilt and shed
is to pray, to turn to mulch
is to pray, to stretch in the dark
is to pray, to break surface
after great months of ice
is to pray, and to squeeze love
up the stalky center toward the sky
with only dreams of color
is to pray, and finally to unfold
again as if never before
is to be the prayer.

CARVING THE RAFT INTO A FLUTE

Given sincerity, there will be enlightenment.
—*The Doctrine of the Mean, 200 B.C.*

Of all the things I've seen
after opening my eyes
hundreds of times a day
for hundreds of days,
any one will do,
for it is in the empty glass
as well as the full, and early light
which is only early to us, warms
the mouth of a simpleton
as well as a scientist,
and the wind up from nowhere
stirs the dead tree as cleanly
as the living.

Of all the things I've thought
while undressing when tired,
the ones that tell me I am alive
have been there all along.
Only something particular
like my lover's far off look at dawn
reminds me that today
is yet to happen.

Of all the times
I thought I liked this
or didn't care for that,

not one was of my choosing
or yours, for as the earth
was begun like a dish breaking,
eternity is that scene slowly
reversing, and you and I
and the things we are drawn to
are merely the pieces of God
unbreaking back together.

EARTH PRAYER

O Endless Creator, Force of Life, Seat of the Unconscious,
Dharma, Atman, Ra, Qalb, Dear Center of our Love,
Christlight, Yaweh, Allah, Mawu,
Mother of the Universe...

Let us, when swimming with the stream,
become the stream...
Let us, when moving with the music,
become the music...
Let us, when rocking the wounded,
become the suffering...

Let us live deep enough
till there is only one direction...
and slow enough till there is only
the beginning of time...
and loud enough in our hearts
till there is no need to speak...

Let us live for the grace beneath all we want,
let us see it in everything and everyone,
till we admit to the mystery
that when I look deep enough into you,
I find me, and when you dare to hear my fear
in the recess of your heart, you recognize it
as your secret which you thought
no one else knew...

O let us embrace
that unexpected moment of unity
as the atom of God...
Let us have the courage
to hold each other when we break
and worship what unfolds...

O nameless spirit that is not done with us,
let us love without a net
beyond the fear of death
until the speck of peace
we guard so well
becomes the world...

LET'S VOICE THE POSSIBILITIES

Let's admit it. In a world filled
with mystery and ruin, we can leave
the house certain of who we are
and return, fatigued by the traffic,
only to have some hidden spirit
howl in our ear, "If you let me live,
you will taste the sweetest part
of being here."

And the next day, we can remember
something essential while fiddling
with the radio at a stop light.

So, let's voice the possibilities.
If you fly, you will be seen,
for your wings are powerful
and colorful. If not, you will
miss why you are here.

What does it mean to fly? Well,
that's the question, isn't it?

For those wanting to be loved,
it is the courage to say,
I am lonely.

For those tumbling in their fear,
it is the courage to accept
that nothing is certain
but still to know
in this open wing
that is your breath
that you are safe.

Things No One Asks About

I have been called heroic
for merely surviving.
It's like championing an eagle
for flying to its nest

and I have been condemned as selfish
for following the call of truth
which is like blaming a turtle
for finding the deep

and I have escaped death more than once
but not the dying.

*

I have been worn slowly by experience
and torn apart instantly by crisis and revelation
and all I can say is Life is Food:
to love is to chew; to forgive,
to swallow.

I cough up these bits:
that the heart like a wing
is of no use tucked

and distrust in the world
like an eye swollen shut
stops the work of love.

*

Like a worried glassblower
trying to refigure his clear and shattered heart,
I have cut myself on all that I was,
surprised that wisdom hides
in the brilliant edges.

At the Window

I was at the window
when a fly near the latch
was on its back spinning—
legs furious, going nowhere.

I thought to swat it
but something in its struggle
was too much my own.

It kept spinning and began to tire.
Without moving closer, I exhaled
steadily, my breath a sudden wind
and the fly found its legs,
rubbed its face
and flew away.

I continued to stare at the latch
hoping that someday, the breath
of something incomprehensible
would right me and
enable me to fly.

THE GREAT OPENING

Act always as if the future of the Universe depends on what you do, while laughing at yourself for thinking that whatever you do makes any difference.

— *Buddha*

I want to learn more and more to see as beautiful what is necessary in things, then I shall be one of those who makes things beautiful.

— *Nietzsche*

KNOWING, DRINKING AND SEEKING

Without knowing who I am—
that is, without finding the place
where God and I join—I will
become everyone I love.

Without drinking from the quiet—
that is, without listening for the place
from which all living things speak—
I will talk too much and wonder
why I am not heard.

Without seeking the self that lives
beneath all names, all my attempts
at kindness will fail, for everything
I do will turn everyone in need
into me.

This being human is a series of
blindnesses that come and go.
But we can outlive our mistakes.

The mysterious river is always
near and greater than our thirst.

Tu Fu's Reappearance

Out of the yellow mist
he came again, his oriental beard
in tow. We were on a healthy shore
and he sat cross-legged in the sand,
scratching delicately with a branch,
his slender head down. I crouched
and put it to him, "How do I block
the fear?" He kept scratching the sand
as if he hadn't heard. I grew angry,
"How do I block the fear?!" He lifted
his head and shrugged,
branch waving above him,
"How does a tree
block the wind?"
With that, he
disappeared.

THE AFTERMATH OF RAIN

Something below all my conscious desires, something like an impulse that ties me to a tribe of inner sayers, something beneath all doubt knows with every fiber that I must look or I will die. This pulse, at the cellular level of my soul, is what makes me investigate everything with passion. This pulse makes me speak to you. It makes me stand before small gatherings and utter my deepest questions before strangers who once hearing are no longer strangers. And once we become our questions, then the voicings now heard circle the voicings unheard and a delicate music is begun that is both open and secret at once. In the silence that follows, it is unclear who is speaking and who is listening...

I must look or I will die. It is somehow written in my heart. I must say what I see or I will not be fully alive. No one taught this. In truth, each of us, in our own quiet way, is born to dance the unseeable out of the ordinary days, striking our inwardness like a continual drum that somehow keeps the soul of the world going. As if the eternal waits for each spirit to stretch its consciousness over its heart. All of us, like it or not, are seers and sayers who must keep drumming what is in out. All of us blessed and cursed to keep the feet of God moving.

GEMSEED

Loving yourself is like
feeding a clear bird
no one else can see.

You must be still and offer
your palmful of secrets
like delicate seed.

As she eats your secrets
no longer secret
she glows
and you lighten
and her voice
which only you can hear
is your voice
bereft of plans.

And the light
through her body
will bathe you
till you wonder
why the gems in your palm
were ever fisted.

Others will think you crazed
to wait on something
no one sees.

But the clear bird
only wants to feed
and fly and sing.

She only wants
light in her belly.

And once in a great while
if someone loves you enough
they might see her rise
from the nest
beneath your fear.

WITH GREAT EFFORT

There was a huge stone between them.
For a while, each thought the other had
brought it, but it was there long before
them. Neither could budge it, but
together they could rock it a little.

So, with great effort, they rocked it enough
to create a dark space between the stone and
the earth it had packed for so many years.
They could have walked away, but somehow
they knew: if they did, it would always be
between them. So they kept rocking and
wedging, believing there would be a
tipping point. And on the third morning,
the huge stone, like the heaviest of tongues,
finally rolled over with a thud they could
feel in their throats, its underside dark
with clumps of soil and broken roots.
In its unearthed cavity, worms and bugs
scurried from the light. Breathing heavily,
they stared at the huge unearthed thing,
and smiled.

Now, they began to roll it enough
to fit a broken bough beneath it. This,
too, took enormous effort. But very slowly,
they were able to lift the heavy thing
between them, roll it slightly on a branch
of a dead tree, and do it again. And again.

And again. This work went so slow,
it seemed a way of life. But in this way,
they moved the unearthed thing across
a field to the mouth of their garden.

It was here that they washed
the thing that was between them,
but which was there long before them.
Here, they washed it clean of clumps
of earth and insects hidden in the cracks.
Once clean, they could see the veins
in the stone hidden for so long. They were
really quite beautiful. So they pressed
their tired palms to the veins in the stone
and closed their eyes in a form of
unexpected prayer.

Then, they rolled the washed
unearthed thing one last time and where
it landed, they began a path, and this
huge thing, which no one before them
could move, became the first stone.

Though they seldom speak of it,
those who hear the story somehow know
that this is how what seems immoveable
becomes a foundation.

BEFORE THE TWICE-LOCKED GATES

*I come to you from a land where elders have shown their grand-
children how to sing their way through. I write this in a land
where skin pounds skin. From the outside in, we call this brutal-
ity. From the inside out, we call this song. The gift of Africa tells
us that song is the only thing that can outlast brutality. Whether
you suffer an unjust system or an oppressive father, whether you
have been in a prison of another's making or in a cage of your
own construction, this sun-baked continent that carries the
tremor of the beginning tells any who will listen that song is the
only thing that can outlast brutality. The drums, if leaned into,
will carry you along. The drums, which have no beginning or
end, will circle you through the many faces of pain and joy. The
drums sound the heartbeat of God, clear and unending. Even
when oppressed to the point of silence, the drumbeat cannot be
silenced. Even if you are born a funé, a storyteller who is not
permitted to sing, there is song in how you raise your eyes to the
unwatched sky. Even if you are forbidden to cry your truth, there
is the Geuca Solo, the dance without words before the twice-
locked gates. Pain held in is pain. Pain let out is dance. Worry
held in is worry. Worry let out is the cry of a bird that lives on
the branch of heart that no one sees. Sorrow held in is sorrow.
But sorrow let out is the song of the continents moving togeth-
er. Even if you are forbidden to cry your truth, there is still the
dance without words before the twice-locked gates. No matter if
the gates are generations old, no matter if the gates are in your
mind, no matter if when you move, you stumble. It is the gift of
Africa for the children of the earth: God is the wood of the
drums, drums sound the heartbeat of the living, song is the thing
that will outlast brutality...*

TIDAL

I have held the dying,
have felt their life surge one last time
like a surf, have held those not even
a day old, have seen their eyes flicker
out of focus at the coolness
of this thing called air,
and I have been the dying,
held until I came back.

I have been crushed to center
and left for invisible, and played
like a sweet thing with broken strings,
and in the hush after truth is shared,
in the wake of all explanation and excuse,
in the aftermath of illusions snapped
like sticks, nothing matters now
but the instant where all I am
mounts like a wave for you,
the instant my hand parts
the air between us.

I tell you I have come so close
to death that I forgot my name
and now all names seem useless.

So nothing matters but emptying
until the softness we call spirit bubbles
through the tongue and words fail
in utter adoration. Nothing now
but this need to be... naked
in the midst of what we feel.

THE GREAT OPENING

It was the son of a soldier,
a soldier who killed his own people.
It was that gentle son who went
in despair to his grandfather's
bridge to ask in his
solitude why.

And that night he dreamt
that everyone who had been hurt
and everyone who'd done the hurting
met on that bridge. And in their
awkwardness and pain, it began
to rain flowers which grazing
their skin opened their faces
and they were healed.

And the flowers, falling
into the water, brought
the fish who thought
the petals were food.

And the son of the soldier
woke committed to the building
of bridges and to the food
of flowers raining
from the sky.

Utterance-That-Rises-Briefly-From-The-Source

Peace is an odd word for the bubble of all there is
breaking repeatedly on the surface of the heart,
but I know of no other. The Native Americans
come closest; nothing between inner events
and what to call them. I see you and you always
glow. Why not call you One-who-shines-like-a-
sun-upon-first-meeting. Why not call the moment
of doubt and fear: Dark-point-spinning-loose-
that-presses-on-the-throat. Why not call the
moment of certainty, the fleeting moment
when everything that ever lived is right
behind my pounding heart, why not call
that moment: Beat-of-the-thousand-wings-
of-God-inside-my-chest. When I feel love so
deeply that I can't bear it, when I feel it so much
that it cannot be contained or directed at any one
thing or person, why not call it: The-stone-at-the-
bottom-of-the-river-sings. Why not call you: The-
hand-that-plucks-me-from-the-bottom-of-the-river.
Why not call this miracle of life: The-sound-that-
never-stops-stirring-the-lost-within-the-sound-that-
never-stops-soothing-the-living-within-the-sound-that-
never-stops-sounding-in-the-eyes-of-dead-things-coming-
alive-again-and-again-and-again…

BEING A FEATHER

He sat quietly
as his father went silent.
Sometimes, his father
would look far off and
the shape of his eyes
would sag, and he knew
his father was carrying
the things that burn
where no one can speak.

It was then that the feather
appeared. He tried to guess
if it was hawk or crow or
maybe heron, but his father
said, "It doesn't matter
from which flying thing
it comes. What matters
is that it carries us back
and forth into the life above
and the life below."

His father held the feather
as if it were his own,
"It carries us into sky life

and ground life until
both are home."

His father placed the feather
in his hands, "Anything
that connects above and
below is such a feather.
The quiet is such a feather.
Pain is such a feather.
Friendship is such a feather.
The things that burn
where no one can speak
is such a feather. You
are such a feather."

LETTER HOME

You ask if anything's changed.
I write this in an open boat
in the middle of a lake
which has been drawing me
to its secret for months.
I am becoming more like water
by the day. The slightest brace
of wind stirs me through.
I am more alive than ever.
What does that mean?
That in the beginning
I was awakened
as if a step behind,
always catching up,
as if waking in the middle
of some race that started
before I arrived, waking
to all these frantic strangers
hurrying me on,
as if landing in the middle
of some festival not knowing
what to celebrate, as if
someone genuine and beautiful
had offered to love me
just before I could hear
and now I must find them.

You ask if anything's changed.
I am drifting in the lake

and now it's a matter of slowing
so as not to pass it by.

You say I don't sound the same.
It's 'cause I think more like a fish
and only surface to eat.
I used to complain so much,
annoyed that every chore
would need to be done again,
that the grass would grow back
as soon as I'd cut it. Now
I am in awe how it will grow
no matter what you do to it.
How I need that knowledge.
You say I don't try as much with you.
It's 'cause you still behave
as if life is everywhere
but where you are
and I need new knowledge.

It has not all been pleasant.
One of us died the other day.
The last time I saw him,
we held hands through a park fence—
he was thin—but we held as if
the fence weren't there and as if
he were already on the other side.
Now I pray for him anyway, imagining
peace a lighter affair once gone
like pebbles sinking softly underwater.

I put my palm on the water's surface
lightly, not trying to hold any of it,

just feeling it push back.
You ask and I hesitate.
It seems everything has changed
when, in fact, it is only me.

I was closed so long, I thought
opening was breaking and in rare
broken moments I've seen now
how your secret is my secret
just swallowed at a different time
about a different face
with a different though equally
private name that brings it back,
too keenly, too deeply.

I write this in an open boat
where yards from me the heron
perched on turtle rock is spreading
its wings in the sun, holding
perfectly open and still,
the light filling, glazing its eye.
I am drifting here, heart spreading
like a heron's wing, more alive
than I thought possible.
You think me indifferent.
I want this for you
more than you can dream.
I am here. Drifting.
Come. Please. Swim.
If you can.

FOR THAT

How could I know
creating and surviving
were so close

a membrane apart,
a pulsing, glowing film.

How could I know
each day
is
the last
and
the first

and beneath
that tension,
if we wade below it
like the surface
of a sea, a chance
only coral
can feel

and there
we grow
so thoroughly
that breaking
and healing,

creating
and surviving,
first and
last are
one, the
same.

There,
beneath
the tensions
of psychology,
beneath the
pockets of doubt,
beneath the
prospect of
days to be lived
or not lived,

a moment
so calm
it is
cleansing

and I smile
through my
whole body
just to have
a body,
just to have
this orchestra

within that plays
to no conductor.

Will you believe me then,
that like the zen monk
who finds wisdom
in his fears,
who hears more
than he can say,

will you believe me
that no matter what
is shucked or diagnosed
or bled, I would
trade places
with no one,
spirits
with all.

My purpose,
at last,
to hold
nothing
back.

My goal:
to live
a thousand years,
not in succession,
but in every
breath.

SUITE FOR THE LIVING

SUITE FOR THE LIVING

1. ENDGAME

Death pushed me to the edge.
Nowhere to back off. And
to the shame of my fears,
I danced with abandon
in his face. I never
danced as free.

And Death backed off,
the way dark backs off
a sudden burst of flame.
Now there's nothing left
but to keep dancing.

It is the way
I would have chosen
had I been born
three times
as brave.

2. Tell Me You Have Come

There is a timing
larger than any of us, a
readiness that comes and goes
like the heat that makes
our secret walls melt.

How many times have I passed
exactly what I need, only
noticing the stream
when troubled by thirst.

The mystery is that whoever
shows up when we dare to give
has exactly what we need
hidden in their trouble.

3. ADVICE THAT'S HARD TO TAKE

When you pace at the edge of life,
worried and afraid, mount your will
like an arrow of salt
and plunge into
the ocean of experience.

4. ACEQUIA

Only when the fish let go
their dream of having arms
did they grow their magnificent fins.

5. PRACTICING

As a man in his last breath
drops all he is carrying

each breath is a little death
that can set us free.

6. FREEFALL

If you have one hour of air
and many hours to go,
you must breathe slowly.

If you have one arm's length
and many things to care for,
you must give freely.

If you have one chance to know God
and many doubts, you must
set your heart on fire.

We are blessed.

Each day is a chance.
We have two arms.
Fear wastes air.

GRATITUDES

Much of a poet's life is spent hunting out glimpses of a source too big for words, and yet nothing else seems worth sharing. And so, my gratitude to those who have loved me with their patience, even when things were slow in making sense. Deep gratitude to the Fetzer Institute for its support through the years, and to all my colleagues there. And a special bow to Bread for the Journey, a tribe of givers scattered across North America. Their simple devotion to giving, person to person, is an inoculation against the strain of greed that grows within our culture. And how can I thank Marianna Cacciatore, Brandy Sacks, and Wayne Muller for the generosity of their belief and encouragement. And to my friend of the long journey, Robert, I owe so much to what opens when we're together. And to my wife, Susan, who loves me when I put all I know and don't know down. Your heart is a great teacher. Finally, to my reader, you are always alone and never alone. As am I. May these poems be threads by which we find each other.

—MN

ABOUT THE AUTHOR

Mark Nepo *is a poet and philosopher who has taught in the fields of poetry and spirituality for thirty years. Nominated for the Lenore Marshall Poetry Prize, he has written several books, including* The Book of Awakening, Acre of Light *(also available as an audiotape from Parabola under the title* Inside the Miracle*),* Fire Without Witness, *and* God, the Maker of the Bed, *and the* Painter. *He has also contributed to numerous anthologies.* The Book of Awakening *was a finalist for the 2000 Books for a Better Life Award, and was cited by* Spirituality and Health Magazine *as one of the Best Spiritual Books of 2000.* Unlearning Back to God, *a collection of Mark's published essays from 1985-2004, is due out from Khaniqahi Nimatullahi Publications (London, Fall 2005). His most recent books of poetry are* Suite for the Living (2004) *and* Inhabiting Wonder (2004), *both available from Bread for the Journey (www.breadforthejourney.org). His new book,* The Exquisite Risk, *is due out from Harmony Books (New York, Feb 2005).*

As a cancer survivor, Mark remains committed to the usefulness of daily inner life. Through both his writing and teaching, he devotes himself to the life of inner transformation and relationship, exploring the expressive journey of healing where the paths of art and spirit meet. For 18 years, Mark taught at the State University of New York at Albany. He now serves as a Program Officer and Poet-in-Residence for the Fetzer Institute in Kalamazoo, Michigan, a non-profit foundation devoted to fostering awareness of the power of love and forgiveness in the emerging global community. He continues to give readings, lectures, and retreats.

ABOUT
BREAD FOR THE JOURNEY INTERNATIONAL

Bread for the Journey International is a non-profit organization dedicated to nurturing the natural generosity of ordinary people. We believe that our natural impulse is to be generous, to be useful and kind in our families and communities.

Within our 21 regional chapters, we nourish a simple practice of neighborhood philanthropy. In turn, each volunteer-run chapter offers a unique blend of practical assistance, funding and encouragement to help people in their local communities start valuable new projects quickly and easily — without complicated grant proposals and lengthy waiting periods. As a result, countless dynamic programs — ranging from arts to education to relieving poverty — are being born that heal and nourish communities in ways that are naturally creative and responsive to local culture.

Mark Nepo has generously offered two books of poetry — sold exclusively through Bread for the Journey International — as a fundraiser for our organization. They are titled Inhabiting Wonder *and* Suite for the Living.

To learn more about Bread for the Journey International, to start a chapter or make a contribution, visit our website at: www.breadforthejourney.org

We can be reached at:
Bread for the Journey International
267 Miller Ave.
Mill Valley, CA 94941
415-383-4600

BOOKS BY MARK NEPO

The Exquisite Risk, *February 2005, Harmony Books, NY, NY.*
Spiritual Philosophy, Non-fiction, 304 pp., hardcover.
ISBN: 1-4000-5177-0 / 21.00
1-800-733-3000
http://www.harmonybooks.com/crown/catalog/results.pperl?authorid=57669

Suite for the Living, *September 2004, Bread for the Journey,*
Mill Valley, CA. Poetry. 80 pp., paperback.
ISBN: 0-9760575-1-4 / 16.00
415-383-4600
www.breadforthejourney.org/mark.htm
bjourney@pacbell.net

Inhabiting Wonder, *September 2004, Bread for the Journey,*
Mill Valley, CA. Poetry. 80 pp., paperback.
ISBN 0-9760575-0-6 / 16.00
415-383-4600
www.breadforthejourney.org/mark.htm
bjourney@pacbell.net

The Book of Awakening, *May 2000, Conari Imprint, Red Wheel / Weiser,*
Boston, MA. A Spiritual Daybook, 435 pp., paperback.
ISBN: 1-57324-117-2 / 16.95
1-800-423-7087
orders@redwheelweiser.com?subject=orders

Inside the Miracle, *May 1996, Parabola Audio Library,*
656 Broadway, NY, NY, 10012.
with music by Therese Schroeder-Sheker
Audiotape, 2 cassettes (120 minutes) / 15.95
1-800-560-MYTH www.parabola.org/commerce.php?cat_key=4

Acre of Light: Living With Cancer, *1994, Ithaca House Books,*
Greenfield Review Press 2 Middle Grove Road, Greenfield Center,
NY, 12833. Poetry. 68 pp., paperback.
ISBN 0-87886-138-6 / 9.95
518-584-1728
Also available through www.bibliofind.com and www.amazon.com

Fire Without Witness, *1988, British American Ltd. Out of print.*
Epic Poem. 406 pp. hardcover with color prints.
ISBN 0-945167-06-7 / 22.95
Limited availability through www.bibliofind.com and www.amazon.com

God, the Maker of the Bed, and the Painter, *1988, Ithaca House Books,*
Greenfield Review Press, 2 Middle Grove Road, Greenfield Center,
NY, 12833. Poetry. 101 pp., paperback.
ISBN 0-87886-128-9 / 9.95
518-584-1728
Also available through www.bibliofind.com and www.amazon.com